This Journal Belongs To

....

Made in the USA
Las Vegas, NV
06 January 2022

40418783R10073